Felter

Animals with Pouches—The Marsupials

Animals with Pouches– The Marsupials

BY GERALDINE SHERMAN

DRAWINGS BY LORENCE F. BJORKLUND

Holiday House, New York

Library of Congress Cataloging in Publication Data

Sherman, Geraldine.
    Animals with pouches.

    Includes index.
    SUMMARY: A brief introduction to the physical
characteristics and habits of a variety of marsupials.
    1. Marsupialia—Juvenile literature.   [1. Marsupials]
I. Bjorklund, Lorence F.   II. Title.
QL737.M3S53   599'.2   77-27592
ISBN 0-8234-0324-6

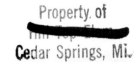

About the Marsupials

The kangaroo is not the only animal that has a pouch. There are many more. Some are as small as a mouse. Others are taller than a human being.

The animals that have pouches are called marsupials. Pouches play a very important part in their lives. After the young are born, they crawl up into the pouch where they can get bigger and stronger. There they drink their mother's milk. They stay there until they are big enough to eat and walk by themselves.

9

10

Australian Jumper

A young kangaroo is called a joey. When it is born, its mother helps it to get into the pouch. She bends over to lick her fur. This makes it easier for the infant to crawl up. It is only as big as a human thumb. For the first few months, it stays in the mother's pouch. But it learns very fast. Soon it will be able to hop out. If danger is near, the mother calls it to come back. She has to lean forward to let the joey back in the pouch.

A Small Kangaroo

A boodie is also known as a rat kangaroo. Sometimes an accident happens before the joey is ready to leave the pouch. It may not live. But the mother has another embryo—an undeveloped young one—inside her. It is very small. While the joey is still using the pouch, the embryo doesn't grow any further. If the joey lives, the embryo will no longer be needed. It will leave the mother's body. But if the first joey dies, the embryo will continue to grow. Soon it will take the place of the first joey. This kind of reproduction is found in most kangaroos.

A "Cat" That Isn't

The young tiger cat (which isn't related to cats at all) lives in a pouch much smaller than the pouch of a kangaroo. A piece of skin shaped like a half moon covers the opening. The infant grows to about one meter long—some three to four feet. It isn't afraid of anything. When it is searching for food, it chases whatever it can find. It doesn't really care what it is. Quickly it finishes the meal and is off to look for more.

Little Acrobat

THE TUAN

A female tuan has a shallow pouch shaped like a saucer. It is not very deep, and only a little edge on it keeps the infant from falling out. It stays inside for the first four months of life. By the time it is a year old, it will have its own young. The adult tuan is a little acrobat. It can twist and turn in the air. Just as easily as it can walk, it flips itself over backward. It likes to go from one branch to another in this way.

14

A Miniature Bear

A wombat's pouch is upside down. The infant holds on with its mouth so it won't fall out. The mother's strong muscles also protect it. When it gets older, it will have only four front teeth. The backs of them are soft. Thus they wear down quickly in back, leaving the front part razor-sharp. They keep growing all the time. A wombat can eat bark and roots easily with its strong teeth.

Piggyback Rider THE KOALA BEAR

A koala bear's pouch is also upside down. When the infant is about six months old, it climbs onto its mother's back. It rides piggyback until it can walk by itself. But the koala goes back into the pouch to sleep and eat. Finally the mother gets the young one used to eating eucalyptus leaves. First she gets rid of her body wastes. Then she releases partly digested leaves. The infant, leaning from the pouch, licks this from its mother's body. A koala smells like cough drops, which contain oil from these trees. These leaves are the only thing it ever eats.

A Banded Termite-Eater

THE NUMBAT

The little numbat does not have a deep pouch to crawl into. It is just a hollow spot underneath its mother. It never lets go of her fur. If it did, it would drop to the ground. When it gets bigger it will hunt for termites. They are its favorite food. Its sticky tongue is so long, it is easy to reach them. The tongue shoots out into a piece of rotten wood. The termites get stuck on it. The numbat eats thousands of these insects at every meal.

Food-Storer   THE FAT-TAILED DUNNART

The fat-tailed dunnart has a small pouch too. When the infant is on its own, it is a mighty hunter. It stands on its back legs to look all around. It sniffs the air for danger. Quietly it sneaks through tall grass, searching for food. When it catches a meal, it eats and eats. But its body cannot use all the food at once. Part of it is stored in the tail, in the form of fat. Some other time the dunnart might not be so lucky in finding food. Then its body has to use the extra food. When it is all gone, the tail becomes thin again.

Tree-Sitter

The spotted cuscus is kept tucked inside its mother's pouch. There it is warm and safe. When it grows bigger, it climbs out by itself. It spends all its life in trees. During the day it sleeps, sitting up, and hunts food at night. When it finds some, it wraps its tail around a branch and sits down again to eat. The fur on its bottom actually wears down from so much sitting.

Desert Digger

Fully grown, a marsupial mole (which isn't really a mole) could fit into a human hand. There is only one infant born at a time. It is blind. The eyes are hidden under muscle and skin. But it doesn't have to see. It spends most of the time digging tunnels underground, looking for earthworms and insects to eat. It is hard for this animal to move—it has to drag itself along. The dirt caves in after it, so it is always making new tunnels. Sometimes it comes out on the surface. But it doesn't spend much time there. Soon it will start digging again.

A Nectar-Eater

The female noolbenger's pouch is near her stomach. If she spreads her back legs, a small infant can be seen. The noolbenger is an unusual mammal, for it takes nectar from flowers, somewhat like a hummingbird. It does this with its tongue, which is almost half the length of its body. It darts its tongue into the nearest blossom. When it is covered with nectar, it is pulled back. The roof of the noolbenger's mouth has wrinkles in it on which the food is wiped off. Then it's ready to get some more.

A Galloping Mouse

When an infant wuhl-wuhl sees the world for the first time, it wants to know all about it. It is full of curiosity. If it finds something new, it stands up on its hind legs. It looks over the new object carefully. Its nose twitches from side to side. Then it comes down on all four feet. But it doesn't jump away— it gallops.

An American Marsupial

When an opossum is born, it is extremely small. A teaspoon would hold 20 of them. The mother watches as the infant struggles to reach her pouch. But she never helps it. When it is old enough, it comes out of the pouch for the first time. Then it clings to its mother's back with its paws and rides about on her, next to its brothers and sisters. It wraps its tail around anything close by, such as her ears or nose. This helps it to stay on top of her. The opossum is the only marsupial found in the United States.

Another Rider

THE RINGTAIL POSSUM

A young ringtail possum—which isn't closely related to the American *o*possum—also rides on its mother's back. The tip of its tail is twisted into rings. It uses this like another paw. When the youngster climbs trees, it wraps its tail around a branch. This keeps the possum from falling off. At the same time, its toes are grasping the limb tightly. The big toe can turn inward like the thumb on a person's hand. This makes it easy for the young one to hang on.

An Animal "Kite"

THE GREATER GLIDER

The female glider's pouch can be seen from below as she soars through the air. The infant rides on its mother's back after leaving the pouch. Soon it learns how to travel from tree to tree. But it doesn't really fly. It glides through the air much like a kite. With its front and back legs spread wide, it leaps off a branch. This makes a fold of skin stretch out between its legs and body. This skin helps it to glide on the air currents.

A Fearless Meat-Eater

THE TASMANIAN TIGER

The Tasmanian tiger's scientific name, *Thylacinus cynocephalus*, means "pouched dog with a wolf head." It is not a tiger, a dog, or a wolf. But it is a bit like all of them put together. Like a tiger, it has stripes. It runs on tiptoes as dogs do. It looks rather like a wolf. At one time these animals were heavily hunted. Most of them were killed. Nobody is sure if any are still alive. It is thought that a few may be safely living in a place where no human can harm them.

A Galloping Marsupial

THE LONG-NOSED BANDICOOT

The long-nosed bandicoot has a pouch that opens between her back legs. New infants are usually born before the older ones leave. Then the pouch gets rather crowded. The infants have to squirm between the others. Soon a young bandicoot goes out by itself. It searches the woods for insects. If something surprises it, it immediately jumps straight up in the air. Then it turns around and speeds away.

There Are Many Marsupials

These are just a few of the marsupials alive today. There are about 200 different kinds. Most of them live in or near Australia. Others are found in South America. Modern marsupials are one kind of mammals, or hairy, milk-producing animals, that began long ago. Some marsupials date back to the dinosaur age, millions of years past. It's good they're still here, for they are among the most interesting animals in the world.

Index

DATE DUE

OC 24 '85		
NO 20 '85		